Night Vision

Night Vision

Christopher Levenson

QUATTRO BOOKS

The publication of *Night Vision* has been generously supported by the Canada Council for the Arts and the Ontario Arts Council.

Author's photograph: Oonagh Berry
Cover image: Sigrid Albert
Cover design: Sarah Beaudin
Editor: Allan Briesmaster
Typography: Grey Wolf Typography

Library and Archives Canada Cataloguing in Publication

Levenson, Christopher, author
    Night vision / Christopher Levenson.

Poems.
ISBN 978-1-927443-58-3 (pbk.)

    I. Title.

PS8573.E945N53 2014   C811'.54   C2014-900573-3

Published by Quattro Books Inc.
Toronto, ON

info@quattrobooks.ca
www.quattrobooks.ca

Printed in Canada

As always, for Oonagh

Contents

Night Vision

STATIC

As a kid before transistors or plastic, I remember
hearing the BBC news on our brown wooden Murphy,
my father twiddling the knobs to block out the static.
Aged five I think I even recall hearing Chamberlain
declaring war: certainly Churchill's orations
infiltrated my childhood while in distant theatres
allied or enemy soldiers fell, or were burnt alive,
and ancient cities crumbled under high explosives.
But that was far away, I was a child, not guilty
of more than normal indifference.
                                        Now it is all too real.
How dare CNN disturb our dinner table,
soil the new broadloom with tank tracks, ethnic killings?
What right has *The National*
to dump corpses in our backyard without even asking?
In this high stakes video game everything happens at once:
green blossoms of tracer light up the Baghdad night sky,
bombs zero in on Afghan villages, ragged deserters
are slaughtered before our eyes. Where's the remote?
Globalization means watching disasters erupt
in real time ten thousand miles away, and knowing
you cannot lift a finger to help or forestall.
If you're not already dead, you're an observer.

PARIS, 1919

for Margaret MacMillan

For six months in Versailles in their
stove-pipe hats, long frock coats and longer faces
Lloyd George, Clemenceau, Wilson,
people in glass palaces, hurl foundation stones
for a lasting peace
across still smouldering rubble.

At working lunches, gala dinners,
the main course is always
plebiscites, war debts, indemnities
in countries they never visit.

Between cigars and cognac,
much talk of self-
determination: statesmen gather
to foreclose on bankrupt empires,
fire sales
where everything must go.

It's time for cards on the table,
a whole house of cards,
winner take all.

In corridors, whispered deals,
and all the while in odd corners,
petitioners,
capitulation in hand,
desperate to save
an offshore island here, an enclave there,
remember their constituents –
some stubbled peasant forced

out of his language, a fisherman
denied his shoreline – and accept
for the sake of principle, face,
dragons' teeth to be broadcast
over barren ground:
half a country maybe
is better than no homeland.

So with set squares and protractors,
they divvy up continents,
draw straight lines across deserts,
settle the nomads, establish tribal kingdoms,
blotting spilt blood with sand,
till Arabs and Jews both sue
for breach of promise.

After they did their best,
the whole botched house of cards
came crashing down,
so that we in our turn can watch
in slow motion
a scorpion rectitude,
justice tempered by vengeance.

STATIONS

Departure: my first day-long journey by train
from Euston to Lancaster in the middle of the Blitz.
I am six years old. My father is playing bridge
as we halt for air raid sirens then grind slowly on
through blacked-out cities, bleak, vacant countryside.
Once there, we live only a field away from the LMS line
and attending a school that overlooks the main station,
after class for a penny platform ticket I collect
train numbers for hours. On locomotive footplates
I gaze into furnaces, envious, talk to drivers,
imagine distances.

Granddad lives near Kings Cross, works on the railway.
On my trips into town the map of the London Tube
is tethered into my mind like a spider's web
that shudders with the approach of every train.
I can find my way there in my dreams,
though in war-time I never know
where the emergency stairways will come out
nor what other tunnels riddle this city at night
as underground railways hand on
downed pilots, refugees.

As a teenager after the war I travel abroad
with my school to Switzerland, learn to thread my way
through foreign terminals, decipher smatterings –
Heisse Würstchen, Kaffee, Limonade – the cries
of trolley vendors almost drown out the announcements:
*"The train now standing at Platform One will call
at Austerlitz, Waterloo, Gettysburg, Dunkirk.
Change here for Hastings, Crecy, Thermopylae, Kosovo Polje,
Nanking, Glencoe, El Alamein, Singapore."*
So many stations! How will this journey end?

At last we ease out of the city, glide past vacant lots,
a slaughterhouse, gasworks, back streets that end in walls,
and I think of a sealed train from Geneva to Petrograd,
or those that linked India and Pakistan, freighted with corpses,
and endless cattle cars moving east with their human cargo.

As we near the frontier customs men lock the doors
to the outside world while a disembodied voice
commands us to stay on the train. We are on our own.
Our fellow passengers emaciate into shadow.
At Auschwitz the tracks founder in grass.
Our plume of smoke darkens the countryside.
The sky chokes with ash we shall wear on our foreheads forever.

MAY DAY

At Mežica in '61, I watched
the local circus's high-wire act, as Slovenian miners
gathered for a good time. Today
before Parliament, a 'field full of folk',
singing and chanting slogans, sprawl in the warm air.
Our hopes float up like balloons, almost lost to sight
May Day
beyond the Defence Department roof.
A woman from Poland
speaks of Solidarność, another foreign word
to freight the list of our common history –
Hiroshima, Dresden, Babi Yar, Sakriet, My Lai –
that rumble past our minds like wagons of the white death train
snaking all week through the western United States
laden with warheads.

Workers and churchmen converging
on this green square lament
the delayed Spring of worker participation,
and form a human chain against the Bomb.
A handful only. May Day most citizens
are home, cultivating their gardens, united only
in their need for a car loan or mortgage.

Later that night on TV
May Day
in Moscow, Beijing, East Berlin, Bucharest,
the People's Armies strut past reviewing stands.
Floats follow them bearing rockets, guns, erect at the ready
to enforce brotherhood before it is all too late.

May Day, May Day, May Day....

ONE FINE DAY

'Nagasaki – the sea, the harbour':
How could Puccini have known
that Pinkerton man, dressed in black,
would return to secure his treasure?

Even with her telescope, Butterfly
could not foresee, decades later,
how her Little Boy would come home
with that ultimate American gift of light.

POPPIES

That time of year again: grieving relatives gather
to wonder what might have been, as octogenarians
shuffle towards the cenotaph. Will the line never end?
Flanders Fields, Ypres, Dieppe, – a hundred campaigns
weigh down their chests. As dark suits, bomber jackets,
explode in crimson, I turn away, refuse
the importunate poppies, feeling shame
that I must pass up these tokens, yet knowing
it is not their sacrifice I reject, only
the Pavlovian dogs of war that hounded them
to early deaths. The drug of glory returns
through flashbacks, stays in our system forever.

Meanwhile across three continents
a war that dare not speak its name injects
action heroes into the jungles of
Colombia or the Golden Triangle, strafing away
from helicopter gun-ships, shooting up farmers
who scratched out a meagre living from mountain coffee
then switched to an instant cash crop,
a little white dust, Eldorado
for America's grasping despair: war
is the opiate of the politicians, a photo-op
chance to look tough with 'our boys' up at the Front.

And I who was never there should keep my peace but cannot:
no less for me the shells rip open the dark.
This night vision is mine too, goes over the top in my sleep,
with derelict veterans selling indulgences.

GEOGRAPHY LESSON

So now I know where Dunblane is:
along with a dozen other
anonymous sleepy towns –
Waco, Killeen, Stockton or Hungerford –
content to be average,
they trundle numbingly past me
like freight cars at level crossings
bearing instead of Santa Fe, Southern Pacific
disasters, massacres.

I say the names over like a black rosary, tribute
to the random power of hatred and the gun.
When the floral arrangements have rotted
and the gravestones are grainy with dust
and the survivors have left,
all I can do is remember
that it will happen again,
that the trains will never stop coming.

MEXICO CITY

In the Zona Rosa the dark-tinted glass
of the latest office high-rise reflects back upon
crowded pavements. Beside the airport freeway
monstrous billboards compete
with the blue of jacarandas
that floats over neighbourhood
corner stores, auto workshops
like a pale dream of wealth and liberty.

TROTSKY AT COYOACAN

Not how I had imagined you, even in exile,
a man who once commanded
armies, addressed vast crowds in Red Square,
now reduced outside Mexico City to taking
the kindness of friends at face value and granted
with your wife and only child
the false security of a few yards
of enclosed garden, a modest house, high walls.
After communing with Diego and Frida failed
this became your last retreat, to all appearances
bon bourgeois, writing steadily away
from the big world or by way of relief
busily attending to flowering shrubs and agava
or petting and feeding your rabbits. Such photographs,
proof of simple pleasures, were no match
in death-crazy Mexico for another artist's intrigue:
on orders from afar trusted familiars
struck you down, cut short
a human experiment, destroyed its blossoming.

Yet as they must the seeds persist, tall trees
outlast the heat and pollution, gather their shades to protect
at least your memory, the solace
of a still unrealized dream.

LIKE A HUMMINGBIRD

Like a hummingbird
by the dawn's early light
a bright yellow helicopter
hovers above the embassy's
rooftop landing pad,
biding its time.

THE BALLAD OF THE SILENT WOOD

Men came at night from the silent wood,
knocked at a villager's door,
told two or three to come with them,
they did not say what for.

Hastily dishes were stacked away,
food littered the unswept floor.
They left with hardly a word of farewell,
they never asked what for.

At gunpoint they trudged through the silent wood,
in the half-dark tripped on stones.
Their bare feet stumbled against roots
that stuck up through the earth like bones.

Men, women, children – none was spared.
some whimpered, some were brave.
They stood in line, ten shots rang out,
they dropped to a shallow grave.

And every day for five long years
the killings did not stop
behind a fence three metres high
with barbed wire on the top.

Though pine trees were planted over the pit
where there was so much to hide,
nothing would flourish in that bitter soil,
every sapling withered and died.

Yet in the village no one spoke.
Was nothing seen or heard?
Did no sound escape from the silent wood
where their neighbours disappeared?

On Saturdays, uniformed in black,
strangers came to the village dance.
Some villagers laughed and drank their fill
and took care of the soldiers' wants.

Fifty years more all held their breath
and shunned the silent wood,
from fear that knowing too much might do
neither them nor the dead much good.

Then archaeologists dug out the pits
and questioned the older folk
till a hundred thousand skeletons
re-emerged from the mist and smoke.

Then at last the buried tears could flow
and rage took hold of the hills
and the silent woods grew loud again.
It is the silence kills.

THE SITES OF EL SALVADOR

In the hills of El Salvador
a clutch of archaeologists
crouch in the dirt like kids
around a jigsaw puzzle.

A special UN Commission
is fitting the pieces together
into a massacre.
It recovers collector's items

almost as good as new:
bones, fabrics, shards of skin
from babies thrown in the air
as if by a playful father

then bayoneted as they fell.
Forensic skills unearth
for mothers, their minds gone, hard
evidence of their love,

shredded before them, skulls
holed by three bullets. But some,
hiding in barns, saw it all,
survived, to show and tell.

President Cristiani
claims he would like to protest
such invasions of privacy:
have we no respect for the dead?

With old rumours verified
he proposes an amnesty
'to put the past behind us'.
Elsewhere, remaindered,

his scarecrow officers,
no longer men of action,
are stripped of insignia,
dwindle to rag and bone.

CATCHING UP ON THE NEWS

At dusk we had gathered kindling with the ritual innocence
of campers on day release from cities, trying to match, flame for flame
the lurid sunset over the lake,
crowding around the embers till they died,
then crawling back into the chrysalis
of tent and sleeping bag. Already next dawn
the brilliant blue promises of conciliation
that last night clamped us together in song are ash:
we must return.

For ten days the world was lost
along trails and whitewater rivers where the only rumours
were chipmunks scuffing leaves, the sole danger
aged bears. Now, the car radio on
as we plunge downhill over the toll bridge
into the stink of woodpulp, our ears
cannot take it in, this swelter
of information. The whole imaginable globe
tattoos our minds with disaster.

All is not lovely even
in our neck of the woods. Gazing in forest pools,
our peaceful reflections blocked out the rest of the world
so we could imagine it whole. Why be aware
that the bullfrogs are slowly dying? We cannot taste
the acid in rain refilling the lakes on the Shield
that can no longer protect us. Will smoke signals ever reach
the Nation's Capital? We need
Vesuvius at least. Otherwise who is there
will ever see, who will hear of,
the tree's, the forest's falling?

NEWSREEL

In the news clip from Liberia
the naked running boy,
when shot, did not get up
but lay in the dust quite still.
This was no stunt.
In the film of his life
he was not just an extra,
he played the title role.

SINCERITY

Look into the eyes of jaguar or leopard:
they are so sincere.
As they crunch through the skull
of a gazelle they have just brought down
into the long grass and raise their blood-smeared jaws
from still warm innards,
you can tell they mean it.
Their gaze is so calm and direct,
they enjoy killing.
Likewise Hitler and Stalin:
all the world's great leaders can look firmly ahead
and not see you in the crowd,
not see the crowd.

SNUFF MOVIE

Thanks to *National Geographic* on TV, I can watch
a parade of serial killers:
a cheetah on its haunches stalking a monkey,
creeping closer downwind, then making the leap.
I hear the crunch of his teeth as the jaws get a grip
on neck and skull, so wholly given over to
the task at hand. He drags his prey painfully up
to the crotch of a tall tree, safe from marauders.
Next a gang of hyenas sequesters and circles a springbok
before they gouge the dying body. Finally lion cubs
bound from long grass to bring a zebra down,
then, mouths triumphantly bloody, dispute gut and gristle.
All this we take in our stride – the brief life of animals,
the random pursuit that harries the weak and the sickly –
that we may admire their sleekly purposeful running,
the coup de grace we could never manage ourselves,
and envy such unity, such undivided will.

ZOOS

are the animals' Third World
concrete favela
with all mod cons except freedom.

Here humans are treated to
random bytes of the wild,
aphrodisiac extract of tiger.

Zoo directors do their best
for reluctant school excursions
and family groups, to explain

our vanishing heritage, to show
how creating new subdivisions
will crowd out orangutans, condors,

golden lion tamarinds. A makeshift
half solution, pre-screened
by climatic zones, fences off

desert, tropical, tundra,
protects the sad beasts
from natural predators.

These welfare recipients
get chow, not grubs or tubers.
Living from hand to mouth,

an involuntary clown school
of chimpanzees, lemurs,
jugglers and acrobats,

seem to be paying their way
by turning tricks, panhandling
for nuts and bananas.

As our food chains collapse,
grinning apes throw back
my own complicity,

all this at most a shelter,
a halfway house back to the wild.
The ark is foundering.

NIGHT VISION

After the air-raid siren eerie calm:
assembled thousands waited
alongside Heritage Harbour,
standing as if in homage
while the first fanfares of light
rocketed up, dispensing
euphoria; excess
of red, green, white, blue
burst onto our waking senses;
smattering salvoes
cascaded in free fall
over the flared outline of the West End
and Stanley Park.
                It was a wonder
I had not witnessed in such magnificence
since as a kid I jungled with flagging crowds
on VE Day in Piccadilly Circus.
But this time without noise. Even armadas
of small boats, barges, yachts
moved without sound as a barrage of shells
hollowed our consciousness, let loose
the great unshackled beast of our darkest fears.

For me the war zone around English Bay
brought back to mind Ypres and Passchendaele,
two stations of the cross
en route to nationhood.

Thousands fell too in the trenches
at Srebrenica, all males over fourteen,
hands tied behind their backs, herded together,
machine gunned, while in Sarajevo
mortar shells blasted the market
and scattered limbs were hastily swept up.
This was no way to cauterize
the wounds of history.

Karadjic by all accounts was
a friendly, courteous man, well-liked by neighbours,
a psychiatrist with a bent for the spiritual,
hiding for a decade behind the burka of
a Santa Claus face-saving beard.
With such a benign growth, who'd not assume
a priest-like holiness
in those calm eyes and all the talk of healing?

Thirteen years on, in his own mind,
he still felt the slaughter
totally justified, as needful as
mowing the lawn,
taking out the trash of genocide,
under an assumed name,
ethnic cleansing. For him now
the future also will be
a foreign country.
We have seen too many newsreels
where night vision goggles, trained
on the invisible, equipped
to reveal landscapes, bring us closer
to our enemies, facilitate
the kill, help us see our way
clear-eyed through a maze of horrors
to whatever action is needed

without the lightning flash of explosions
exposing settlements abandoned,
booby-trapped: we are poised
on a crumbling parapet
of time, liable each second
to plunge into the gullies.
These green shadows offer no safety.

Detached from loving homes,
become mere instruments,
we attain kinship, grow one
with hawk, weasel, hyena,
though we gag at what we see
in spite of ourselves.

Even the blindfolds of faith
slip as we look upon
sprawled bodies of children
broken beside women,
old men, wantonly
spilt across lintels, their hearts'
blood defacing the courtyard.
It's a virus we cannot shake
that enters bone and bloodstream,
an unspeakable secret
we have signed on to,
memories and contours of
fear and revulsion at what
we had harboured within us,
what we could force ourselves,
or be forced, to do to strangers,
our fellow humans.
We cannot wait to see
the green flesh withering,
until what once were bodies

cease to accuse
in human shape, transformed
into mere skeletons.

War has become
our only faith, our one
communion. We have seen through
the night and know
it will return.

Habitat

REMEMBERING THE FLOOD

That first day in '53,
on the ferry from Hellevoetsluis,
cramped against hammering metal, hot diesel fumes,
we watched one horizon swaying and another
emerge out of the mist. Slowly we grew accustomed
to a new world of grey water as the almost sunken island
of Overflakkee floated alongside. We clambered on trucks
and were driven in the half-dark along dykes
through Middelharnis to Oude Tonge. Even two months after
the sea's bombardment, it was a war zone:
roofspars of houses exposed to the looting wind,
the polders awash with debris
of absent families, smashed farms. At the relief camp
we cleaned bricks, rebuilt pigsties.
                                    November that year
with the last breach repaired, the pumps beginning,
I returned to other villages, Dreischor, Nieuwerkerk, –
the names blur – cleaning out homes
that reeked from nine months under salt water, disinterring
from beneath the bed stone bottles of Dutch gin
next to the family Bible, scraping the walls free of sea-pox,
scouring wells until the winter made the sand
too hard for digging. Meanwhile in the village
only the mayor and a handful of labourers remained
and the police, working all hours to bring us fresh water.

There were times we escaped
to Zierikzee or the dunes but for the most part
where now wide causeways run we were marooned behind
                                    sandbags,
abiding the onset of winter.
I was nineteen and this my first close look
at human misery, my total immersion.

AT THE CITY'S EDGE

At its frayed edge the city
unravels into wasteland,
industrial zones where everything
is on hold: the spur line's
waiting containers, giant cranes
fronting the factory wharf, the river
stuck at low tide, nothing
unloaded.

Even night hardly blurs
outlines of oil drums, razor wire
standing on guard around
water filtration plants
and as yet unserviced lots.
No one lives here, the place
defines itself by absence, the roads
lead nowhere fast.

On the distant Trans-Canada
sky signs twitch like Morse;
pennants of flame burn off
from oil refineries;
at twenty-four-hour truck stops
stagnant pools of light
dissolve or coalesce.
The scavenging winds lie low.
Where do we go from here?

Reluctant amnesty
before shadows return
and daylight descends like shale
to envelop tarpaper shacks,
fast-food joints on the Strip,
restoring a semblance of colour
to our tenuous holdings,
no longer nature's,
not yet human.

NEW MILLS REVISITED

It seems at first just another
desolate post-industrial
huddle of cottages,
slate roofs straddling the ridge,
but go down into the gullies
gouged out by two swift rivers,
four railway lines and a canal
and you will find the twisted
strands that made up this town:
steam-blasted mills succumb
through a dozen shades of green
to calm antiquity;
the once surrounding slums
are long since overgrown,
nothing remains of their squalor.

Nature assuaged harsh brick,
flowers and weeds overflowed
the viaduct arches, the millrace,
lichen adorns the sills
of broken factory windows.
In the late autumnal woods
drizzle has made its truce,
eased the asperity
of stone, softened the outlines
of rusted machinery,
bestowing on me as I pass
bewildered gratitude.

MARGHERA

Half-hidden from Venice where
bishops are blessing the sea,
this industrial boneyard,
unused for three decades,
is reduced to its elements:
even cement slowly
crumbles, railway sidings
smother in grass,
rib cages of sheds
lie open to the sky
for prowling winds to pick at;
fire escapes leading nowhere
among the viscera
of pipes and catwalks, toxic
holding tanks, gantries,
dynamos, ships' screws:
this skyline etched in acid
was also a blueprint once.

Now the whole sad inventory
is stripped to bare concrete,
mere scrap, perspectives lost,
surplus workers laid off,
ghosts of machinery,
technology dismantled.

A rusty sunset leaks
into the vacant lots,
its colours corrugate
the listless lagoon's grey waters
with unblessed effluvium.

BRANCH LINE

Once a branch line ended here.
Now that sidings, coal merchants' yard,
ticket office and draughty waiting room
have been swept away, there's nothing left to see.

Only local historians could disinter
from under the shrubbery trace elements
of creosoted wood and horse-drawn carts.
'Desirable homes, three bedrooms, bathrooms en suite'
have covered up the mock-Tudor entranceway.
Once a building's gone the eye so easily
forgets, adapts to new patterns.

Unlike memory: though braced, I was still shocked
to find war-time allotments grown into a mall,
the Fighter Command air strip, where I'd watched Lysanders
take off and land, bulldozed and manicured
into a Golf Course and Country Club.

As a child I thought buildings were permanent.
The war put an end to that: though in the mind's
tousled undergrowth I stumble on scars and shrapnel,
there's no one around to share it with and where a V-2
took out a whole row of houses, all has been neatly restored
to the status quo. This is no place for revenants.

DISCONTINUITIES

at the Emily Carr exhibit, Vancouver Art Gallery, May 1988

Daylight pours down upon
villages long since lost.
Though on canvas they are alive,
the totems have been removed,
stowed in museums, the luminous
rain forests clear-cut.

True, there is more light now –
it is steady, mechanical –
but the mysteries are buried,
the potlatch rituals
denied and documented,
and the Nootka have left Haida Gwaii,
crossed the last waters
to the Lower Mainland.

First Nations words survive
in street names, subdivisions,
their history neutralized
in coffee table books.

Evolving the tangible,
you, Emily, explored
secret hinterlands of dream,
took sensual bearings in the undergrowth,
saw into the cedars, saw beyond
branch swirl to hidden presences,
spirit of raven, bear.
From my 1910 'heritage' hotel
on English Bay I walk
to Queen Elizabeth Park

where MacMillan Bloedel's hush money
built a conservatory, brought
beautiful foreign birds
into a man-made wilderness
complete with climate control.

IN THE SMOKIES

Over dinner at the Hemlock Inn, recently featured
in *Beautiful Homes and Gardens*,
a woman with iron-grey hair
proclaims herself a Child of the Depression –
she is an old child now – and lauds the Puritan
virtue of self-reliance. Her self-made husband nods.
Down the road on the Cherokee strip, once part
of a nineteenth-century pioneer lebensraum,
tame Indians, tarted up in feathers, tout
obsolete heritage:
every hot dog stand and craft shop boasts its own
'live bear' in a cage,
or standing bored on parade, begging, a welfare bum,
while twenty feet up on a billboard in his rocking chair
the Colonel dispenses 'good chicken'.

At the parking lot near the Pass, a black bear cub,
bewildered by a dozen Polaroids,
ambles off into the bushes (elsewhere that day
a mother bear routed a gang of noisy hikers
into the rhododendrons) and the proud owners
of fully-equipped Winnebagos stroll back
in cowboy hats with their trophies of the wild.

So much for wilderness! The future lies
in cities, gleaming
evangelical self-made deserts.
The gold the conquistadors sought is all in Fort Knox,
the reserves no longer exist, the past
is honoured only in plaques, the noble savages
slowly poisoned by mercury
are tucked out of sight, behind billboards, under long grass
with the bones of the buffalo. The rest
is history, or silence.

EARTHWORKS: A ROAD POEM

In Iowa, in the mid-Sixties, I saw them everywhere –
earthworks, preparing Interstate 80,
making room for a new civilization:
dinosaur cranes and tractors
with twelve-foot high tires and huge fangs
grubbed up farmland, whole hillsides
disgorged and shovelled, landfill
for waiting dump trucks.

Forty years later the master plan
makes everything conform:
so what, as we drive at sixty,
that highways rip apart
the fabric of the countryside,
that power lines transfix
ancestral burial grounds?
We have become accustomed
to see a stand of pines,
dense forests, blurring into
brief interludes of green, mere cover-up
between strip mall and parking lot.

Fragments of solitude are set
adrift, childhood memories
smoothed down, erased
by the clean lines of bridges,
while a mirage of small towns,
their store fronts glazed with heat,
vanishes in an instant, blown away
like tumbleweed. In a few years
no one's left to recall
how destitute settlements made way
for this hygienic emptiness.

Half-mast America is a land possessed
by ghosts, can only recall its past
as glory. It is a stalled vision,
though constantly cheated
of its first pristine virtues,
still thirsting for absolutes.

As those rear-view snapshots
of glossy prosperity
are cropped, cut down to size,
nothing remains to build on,
no rock bottom. Concrete and tarmac
are never enough.

Where once Carnegies and Fords
blasted their way across
a supine continent, theirs
for the taking, inarticulate grief
now mourns the demands of empire.
Harvested like grapes, the young
are pressed into a heady
sacrifice, far away and in vain,
while, left behind, the old
with their bewilderment
have not yet learned to lie fallow.

INDUSTRIAL ESTATE

Saturday noon: the industrial estate
forsaken for the weekend. I walk through
its functional landscapes – empty loading bays,
flatbed trucks surrounded by chain-link fence.
Everything's stowed away – sound, colour,
diesel fumes. A no-man's-land, uneasy
truce between city and countryside.
                          Along the highway
in winter's first serious snowfall
half-buried stalks of grass, milkweed, are bent
into random calligraphy.

INDIANAPOLIS

Freedom – to what end?
This chaos of freeways
criss-crosses restless America,
flyover, underpass, tunnel and viaduct
consume the city centres.
Between them acres of rust,
truck depots, loading bays,
abandoned foundries. Why
was this standard-issue city
deposited here in mid-Prairie
a hundred years ago?
Why, at whatever speed,
are we still so far from home?

DOWNTOWN CALGARY

Nobody lives here:
this city distils
extracts of pure absence.

Corporate Canada's
thirty-storey high
brutalities
make no concessions to style,
locale, or weather, they are all
mirror.

No one sees where
the power derives:
no stains of oxblood or oil
deface these verticals.

Consume, say the logos,
before it is too late.
Invest, in case by winter
it is already gone,
this glossy, ice-cold
montage of skyway and mall,
these self-contained underground
arterials
that ward off the climate,
evade human contact:
there's no one about on the streets
of this instant ghost town.

HABITAT

for Moshe Safdie and in memory of Lewis Mumford

Prologue

Once everything was distance: as a kid in my London suburb
anywhere else was a house of postcards, balanced
precariously on the words of my father's friends
who came as refugees burdened with stories from Hamburg,
Vienna, Berlin, their desperate homelands, self-stored
'for the duration'. It took till I was eighteen
to find my own way, to know what 'city' meant,
a knowledge that grows within me like rings in a tree
into my age. Now I can turn at will,
wheel back those days when first I explored alone
Munich or Amsterdam, felt on my tongue
the bitter dust of the Balkans, the desolation
of Djakarta's slums or Delhi's,
or the high of my first sighting
of Vancouver and San Francisco, knowing myself to be
part of this city, that era, a succession of nights,
a pulsing anagram of the places I lived through
that strobe my body with memories. Their details re-jig my brain:
the brawl of sun-striped, rain-battered market stalls,
myriad peasant voices arguing,
haggling like seagulls over a scrap of cloth,
a scrag end of mutton; evening's first lamps string out
the curve of the esplanade; the floodlit fortress surveying
the Old Town beyond the stairways and statued bridge,
the cathedral's son et lumière and the ornate piazzas,
a maze of open-air cafés with always the chance of seeing
familiar faces and stopping to chatter a while
over cappuccino or latte. People are on display here.
In Budapest's Vaci Utca, Amsterdam's Kalverstraat,

in every Italian or Jugoslav town towards nightfall
townsfolk converge on the Corso to see and be seen, to enjoy
the pride of being at home to everyone. These cities become me.

1.
Already in early morning the brute
astringent air, the girders of viaducts
brace for the stress of commuter trains, their cards of light
shuffled quickly as with oblique flashes, windows catching the sun
make cryptic morse for their huddled freight of nine-to-fivers
while the haze drifts up from the mountains,
gathering with it the smoke from the harbour.
We are the ones who conspire here, who breathe together,
we are the places we live. For cities have always
given us strength to distinguish elegance, beauty;
such daily scenes temper our knowledge, infusing
the marrow of consciousness: the highly strung resonance
of the Golden Gate Bridge or the Lions Gate, uplifting the heart,
or Brunel's ecstatic lute spanning the Avon
two hundred feet over the gorge,
completing the landscape. These grant me
lasting measures of grace, for how can city walls
not impose on those dwelling within them even now
a dream of coherence, networks of interconnection?

2.
First accept the contradiction, the struggle between
imposed order, organic growth: cities are not utopias
but constant makeshifts, kaleidoscopic shuffling of lives,
a mongrel amalgam. They do not spring fully formed
from the head of Apollo but grow slowly at first
out of the soil from a gathering of plaided clans, haphazard
salvage of shipwreck and landfall, settling beside
a confluence of rivers, a ford, or a natural harbour.
Then steady layering – taverns, chapels, a schoolhouse –
over the centuries builds to

civility, urbanity, words
that imply respect, order and precedence.
But always precarious: history is liquid,
flows downhill like lava towards us, involving
roots, stones, trees, irresistibly destroying
all that tries to withstand, collapsing dreams,
reducing ideals to rubble. Townsteads are shaped by it
and a single hero's defiance against the odds,
the swelling crowds on the plaza finding their own
revolutionary voice at last can only for moments
counter its onrush: settlements, landmarks
in minutes are lost forever and all that remains is detritus,
courtyards and alleys that harbour stray fragments, silt, alluvium.

3.
A city like a poem grows in the mind,
randomly brick by brick, word by slow word builds to climax
and a time when everything in it is alive.
Then, taken for granted, declines as the centre is hollowed
and suburbs take over. No city can remain pure:
whether in skin or corporate sky-sign graffiti,
that vandalize the walls of night with neon, the multicultural
colours will run, the traffic will converge along arterials,
merge and divide into lanes, becoming embodied, part of the
blood flow.
But what took decades or centuries to build traffic grinds down
to dust: whole blocks of the city centre clear-cut, sandstone consumed
by the acid exhaust, the rush hour's incessant convulsive
shove and bluster as buses and eighteen-wheelers
thrust their bulks forward, dinosaurs jostling for space.
Such radical surgery stops the city's heartbeat, but cannot restart it.
Meanwhile on the overhead thruway's sixteen lanes the urgent
truckers
pound through at a hundred, fibrillating. This triple bypass
shakes us all to the core till the patient city expires.

4.

Under this barrage day and night blur, diminish, raw cement
has scarcely dried before the next wave of commuters
arrives from their pasteurized safety. Cities, though, welcome
                                                    surprise –
that sudden knock-down vista of mountains emerging
behind a used car lot, or a corner store tucked away
at the end of a block of standard-issue apartments;
or flowering shrubs bursting upon us like summer hydrants in purple,
vermilion, to redeem the arid stillness; or arguments overheard
at supermarket check-out counters in yet another language
I do not know. This unpredictable city,
subject like trees to wind and soil and erosion, a product
of tributary streams, is a meeting place, melding façades and angles,
tennis court, diner, bank, Union Hall, Sally Ann. Over decades
buildings have grown upon us, like kudzu or Spanish moss, investing
the neighbourhood with airs of permanence, nestling into our minds
as rightfully there. So, though we rarely respond
to the visual clues of cornice or gable or dormer windows, once
a familiar landmark is razed and another erected, we feel it
like the loss of a family member, someone we'd grown accustomed to
having around, accepting his eccentricities,
bad puns, endless stories, and when we look at ourselves
in the mirror of the upstart plate glass emporium we are unnerved.
Who knows what will remain of our past if this won't? This was a
part of our growing. These undistinguished run-down storefronts,
backlane garages and toolsheds may well be for future researchers
all that remains, our heritage not just objects we handed on
preserved but not pristine, but also things we let slip
through our careless fingers, beer bottle tops, foil wrappers,
cigarette packs, wrinkled condoms, a plastic spoon,
to make of what they can. These they will never discover
recorded on the internet but at basement level, buried
under ten feet of dirt. This accident we must live with.
So yes, if you must, devise pedestrian malls, factor in

grandiose congress centres, civic squares, set aside
industrial acres, residential zones,
but if your heart's not in it, if it does not become the people,
if we shy away and are wary
of the high-rise offices' sheer effrontery,
if our paths of desire
do not accord with the prescription park,
it is all to no avail.
Perfect cities repel: Brasilia, Canberra,
designed to be complete with nothing to add,
no assembly required. We have to make them our own,
to gain some purchase on the glossy blueprints.
It can be done.
As even in concrete castings swallows will find their niche,
so humans who need it no less seek places to rest and return to,
a breathing space. Cities with their own lives
don't just lie down and play dead for planners: their people
learn to break free of aesthetic prisons
from Hausmann's boulevards to Ceaucescu's megalomaniac Bucharest
and hazard a modus vivendi. Like a virus we work around
the latest antibiotics and learn to accommodate.

5.
Cities exist in time and at least attempt to be
some pledge of permanence, a will to stay put, to endure.
As London, Dresden, Hiroshima, Jerusalem, Baghdad
they outlast stone or concrete, they survive war. Our real estate
is freedom, to look from another angle, to move on,
and the freedom of cities is given to those who take it
for granted, as their inheritance, who delight in the motley.
Not to be found in property taxes or by-laws, living people
flash out like single windows at sunset against the crass
shadows of totem skyscrapers, conduits of molten gold.
And clearings are allowed for, precincts of quiet, a place
to stand still among the leaves' conspiracy and a small fountain

and old timers at noon playing chess on the public benches.
For this is what fashions where we belong, locality,
creating as if by some whispered password a whole world
of habitual greeting, a smile. We stake a claim
in neighbourhood, this is our home. We are the ones who live here.

SILENCES

for Edward Hopper

How you would have loved
those vacant toll booths
outside the hospital
exposed by a single arc lamp,
the emptiness
of all-night convenience stores,
the bleak concrete expanse
of shopping mall parking lots
abandoned except for the lights
and supermarket logos
staining the darkness!

At 4 a.m. the gas bar's
still comatose. Now and again
from anonymous distant thruways
truckers arrive and depart,
head on to the metropolis, whose glow
erases the horizon
while small-town America is lost
in home-grown wilderness.

SENSORS

All night these thousand points of light –
fire alarms, security systems – like galaxies
stay on, unnoticed, patrolling the darkness:
remote ears and eyes scrutinize, monitor
the techno-universe, ready at the press of a button
to track our random comings and goings.
Always armed and alert, surveillance cameras
periscope into our lives, 24/7.
Bar-coded, we embalm
security, censers obediently swinging
in the grasp of governments, and watch our step.
Interns in neurosurgery, wards of the state,
infected with guilt,
locked into ambivalent safety,
we do not know how much
we do not know.

SECURITY

for Alan Gillmor

An ecumenical crowd,
our heads mostly balding or grey, bowed in reverence
before Brahms or Schubert, otherwise alert
to every nuance or missed note, we gather each July
for a buffet of chamber music,
all-you-can-hear in twelve days,
a hundred and ten items on the concert menu, served up hot
in sundry airless churches.
                                        Meanwhile in the USA
as bodyguards swarm convention halls, 'credible intelligence'
about impending attacks on New York or Washington
raises the stakes to orange, depresses the markets.
Yet here we are oblivious, fleeing office blocks at noon
for a quick swig at a Bach cantata or four-part harmonies
in Christ Church Cathedral. We have no illusions that even
the Canadian Brass could bring down
the walls of Jericho or Manhattan's Babel towers.
As for police sharpshooters here, or razor wire,
forget it: we have retained
Beethoven, Mozart, Dvořák
to provide our security.

ODE TO CDG

(Charles de Gaulle Airport, Paris)

Even more than music, or muzak, an airport
is international, the ultimate
gated community, and if no longer
elite, at least self-sufficient.

With its intersecting spars and high-
tech brushed steel, this is no one's home:
here we are all transients, leafing through magazines,
sprawling on well-designed benches

to catch a few minutes' sleep. It does not work.
Though heart and eye might otherwise rejoice at
the clean lines of boutiques and elegant walkways,
PA warnings, boarding announcements

remind us not to relax. At all hours we know
we are being scanned by hidden cameras,
everything's taken care of, we are protected from contact
with every element except fear, and have nowhere to go.

SNOWBIRDS RETURNING

Aimless they stray through the airport like refugees
still looking for the sunshine, finding only the snow
just where they left it over three months ago.
While beyond the Customs, standing in a frieze

friends gather to welcome them, their eyes
still relish bougainvillea, rose, azalea
sprawled across subtropical courtyards. Like a failure
of nerve this absence of colour. No visual surprise

confronts them as, filtering back, each, welcomed like a child
exiled from happy sleep with hugs and news,
is bundled into waiting cars, but they refuse
comfort, deny this dying winter, stay unreconciled.

SETTLING IN

at the Père Lachaise Cemetery

The city's microcosm, this well-ordered, tidy
suburb of yellowing autumn offers tombs of all sizes
among the lime trees and chestnuts, though even here
the avenues are named for politicians and heroes.

If some arrondissements seem more high class than others
with shade more opulent, serviced lots overflowing
with fresh flowers and immortelles, it's hard to know
from the names on headstones, graced by the same

sprawl of kitschy angels, languidly weeping willows, doves –
though less of all this than I'd expected. It seems
so randomly democratic, a true reflection
of the citizens waiting outside. Granted, the dead

are more easily disciplined than the living; even the rebels,
the social activists, lie quietly here, protesting mouths subdued
by the ultimate painkiller, and so multicultural!
Triumphant black marble boasts Chinese, Armenian, Hebrew.

In family vaults generations of moss, lichen, obliterate
some leading businessmen, generals, public officials.
But what editor, I wonder, decides who makes it
into this anthology of the dead?

Site-map in hand, Oonagh and I, wandering here
only an hour or two, weren't interested in
Jim Morrison, gave Chopin a miss, never found
Maria Callas or Sarah Bernhardt, but it was time enough

to savour the weight of collected absences, to ponder
what remains of Imre Nagy, Poulenc, Edith Piaf.
My wife filched one of Colette's carnations and proffered it
in homage to Oscar Wilde. He would have been touched.

In any case, if there's a next time, if we return,
there are enough distinguished visitors left
whom I want to pay my respects to – Ginette Neveu,
Balzac, Max Ernst, Delacroix, Nerval, Proust –

Will the line never end? Death's a growth industry,
an international combine harvester. For now we move on,
back to the living, but aware as we enter the Metro
that the Underground bides its time, waits to take over the city.

Vox Humana

THE WORKS

Love is a fast food, a finger food.
Taking the drive-thru lane,
grab all you can, eat on the run:
love's a no-stopping zone.

Stuff yourselves with each other:
love is a sacrament,
body and blood to go,
Big Mac and Coke, the Works.

Love is smash-and-grab,
breaking and entering.
Get it all while it's hot,
then hit the road, make a clean break.

Love is the getaway car.

Love is your name in lights
on Broadway, an all-star cast,
a smash hit, the big time,
the tightrope, the trapeze,
swinging out of control
over the crowds, no net.

Love is the vertigo.

Love is a street drug,
an all-time high, to die for,
ecstasy, angel dust.
Even young kids get hooked.

This trip never ends.

THIS IS THE ROCK

To hear the frenzied drummer tell it,
the rampant trombone,
the lead singer grovelling
before his mike,
death is the big taboo,
the ultimate hit single.
That's how you really score.

The faces at the concert etched in acid
are playing at it,
the rhythms that shake them only
heavy petting. Watch them pull out
at the last moment.

But with their heroes –
Janis Joplin, Jimi Hendrix, Brian Jones –
petrified admiration
crowds round them when they go,
when they go the whole way.

NUTRITION

for David Dorken

After victory Aztec warriors would
devour the hearts of brave slain enemies,
partaking of their courage. So now
in a second-hand bookstore I grab like a cannibal
at my late colleague's relics, trepan the skulls,
bend back the spines of a dozen books,
and scoop, hope to acquire
some part of the brain, a hint of the intellect
they went to feed.

BLOODWORK

"Make a fist!", the nurse tells me. As the needle enters
I look away. This extra-virgin first pressing
will be screened for lipids, 'bad' cholesterol.

At the kerbside bystanders make the twisted,
twisting shape 'comfortable'
until paramedics arrive.
But an obstinate, unquenchable fountain
leaks away uselessly, its motor source
too far gone for harvesting. Red-blanketed,
a derelict body is stowed in an ambulance,
all vital signs monitored.

Like the art bank, the blood bank has many
anonymous donors. To give
is better than to receive:
a few moments' surrender
and a test tube, a bottle is full, providing
a chance of life maybe
a chance of death, and until yesterday
no questions asked: prisoners, derelicts,
bartering blood for food, the meltdown
of solid citizens. Blood
is our information highway,
carries its sick freight undetected for years.
In its final stage, with the H for human gone,
the HIV is ivy, strangling the trunks
of the untouchables.

Necrotizing fasciitis: the virus feasts upon
unwilling hosts, four times out of five kills them.
Your own revolting flesh
is torn away, your leg
instant mythology, amputated
as easily as Québec.

As stronger drugs destroy
smallpox, polio, TB,
a New Model Army
storms in with reinforcements.
Haemophiliacs, who have slowly imbibed
their deaths, are making a fist.

It all comes down to this
blood brotherhood, every cell
a microcosm, no one immune
to the bad blood between us.

PHYSICAL

Luminous blue fish like pins and needles
splinter through the aquarium. Stagnant, we sit
undiverted from our pain
by *Life* or *Sports Illustrated*, while our 'turbid ebb and flow'
is drained off, labelled, bottled for later use.

All nursery smiles, a white-sheathed female vampire
accosts my arm with a syringe, draws blood.
I am no more than my specimens, container for vital juices
about to be processed. Man is the raw material.

Like radar bleeps on the screen at Command Headquarters
warning of doomsday rockets, heart and pulse appear
on miniature TVs: I am an instant star. Tomography,
ultrasound, brain scans, the lot: brushed steel, state of the art

panels of high-tech instruments, panels of experts, wait
to interpret the data, to pronounce the sentence
that our minds cannot register
till we re-enter the real, contagious world
and nose back into the waiting room, listless as fish.

MAINTENANCE

It's no one's idea of pleasure, this tedious
dusting and polishing, swabbing the kitchen floor,
cramming the washing machine with dirty linen.
But someone has to do it or else the house
falls apart. And as for the garden!
The weeds never cease, the pruning, the cutting back
that puts us on call all summer. Likewise, the car:
always something to fix or repair, brake shoes or headlamps
or one tire our lives might depend on looking worn...

City councils make sure that elevators
do not stall between floors or plunge down to the basement
nor rusted balconies give way. Railways and airlines routinely
inspect the smallest parts, check for hairline cracks.
Everything needs ongoing attention:
we can take nothing for granted or ferries capsize,
locomotives derail, planes spiral out of the sky
and although at the time it seemed merely an oversight,
someone is always to blame.

Our bodies remain our one freehold, but with warranties
long since expired, and few parts ever replaceable.
Love too demands
a steady buildup of small attentiveness –
if no longer candlelight suppers or florid bouquets –
once in a while some unprompted random act
that proclaims for our ears only, I love you, I understand.

AT THE SHALLOW END

Beyond the water-winged toddlers and little kids buoyant on
inflatable animals,
the sub-teens are at it:
up against the rope, their ritual bravado
ripples the dazzling chlorinated blue.
They are making waves.
They swell in talk, burst in uneasy laughter.

On garish deckchairs their exhausted poolside
parents keep one eye hazily open
as ten-year-old G.I. Joes and Barbie dolls
pad themselves into heroics, flesh out
their future roles, hormones almost audibly
popping like bubble gum. The boys bristling
with caterpillar green water-guns engage
in hand-to-hand combat, gloat or hurl defiance
at hordes of imagined enemies, the girls
whisper, attend to fingernails, tease hair
or adjust unneeded bikini tops, smile
for cameras they are sure will some day be there.

They know they are on the cusp.
Ready too soon, in the wings, they look ahead, frown
or slump like abandoned teddy bears
as mothers urge them half-willingly to dinner
and they are children again.

FLIGHT PATTERNS

In late October
        watching the last of
                the Canada geese
pulse southward
        on steady wings,
                I am reminded of
those many over the centuries
        who vanished westwards,
                immigrants
from rack-renting or famine,
        their cottages torched,
                their native tongue forbidden.
Beyond the clothes they stood up in
        all they had was song,
                a sense of the lost country
sealed in their heads,
        carried like a tune,
                a black box recording
the flight from hunger, pain
        their setting out
                into darkness, the stations
of exile. Only language
        survives for a while at least,
                language and music.
The burden of song
        in bodhran drum, pennywhistle,
                restores that shared past
in the new land
        and drifts the eyes like smoke
                with the colour of rain-scoured slate
and can for a moment lift
        the disconsolate heart
                to dreams of returning

TAFELMUSIK

for Dina and Michael

As in the half-lit dark of the auditorium
a string quartet walks on, bows, sits down,
each player adjusting his stand, tuning her cello,
and there is total silence the moment before,
with an almost invisible nod, an eyebrow raised,
the first downstroke of the violin begins,
so we, seated for dinner, knowing only
that we like each other, have something in common, key
our minds to a common theme –
children, the latest movies, election results,
or memories of travel, recalling
Singapore or New York, the first mad years of marriage,
the emptiness of divorce.
                              Soon now the tempo quickens,
out of the air we pluck
uneasy resonance, a pizzicato
counterpoint, until our hosts' continuo
with a perfectly timed intervention
eases us, conducts us gently back
into adagios, with maybe a searching question
we must pause to accommodate, a thought
that elicits concord, introduces deeper tones,
approval like the long held note of an oboe.

Another turn. The moment cannot last. Abruptly the fiddle's
rococo mockery garnishes serious themes
with puns and wordplay, while serifs and curlicues
highlight the grander outlines in gold leaf,
nonetheless hoping for comment, contradiction,
a bridge passage somehow into a solo cadenza,
some inspired tale of past joy or sorrow.

                                            Suddenly
it is late, dishes are cleared away, counters wiped down, only
liqueurs and coffee remain to embellish farewells
and produce a mellow finish to our words as once again,
taking our leave, we embrace, and brace for the street's
less hospitable sounds – abrasive sirens, the set
faces of strangers – and modulate into silence.

FAMILY PORTRAIT

Just in time for the official start of Spring
the *Ottawa Citizen* displays
a full-page colour spread of someone we all
knew who is now gone,
out for a walk in the snow
with his wife and three young sons.
Like any normal family they pose,
all fitted out with toques and parkas for winter.

A few years earlier, up in the Gatineaus
my own brood likewise stood, distracted
in grainy black and white, all of us still new
Canadians, with a visiting poet friend,
braced for the ritual snapshot.

Despite the paparazzi you were yourself
as at the start we all intended to be.
How can we ever tell
what lurks around the next corner?
Is anyone prepared
for avalanche, tsunami,
earthquake, sudden disease, or children
disowning a parent, unforeseen distances?
Even strolling to the corner store for a quart of milk
sometimes proves fatal.

Yet what we retain of you
are images: a canoer, someone secure
in his own skin and intellect,
and always his own man. That is enough.

LOCAL TIME

for Sean

Jet-lagged in early Fall I devote three days
to rediscover a son who had grown
(three thousand miles) apart.
Non-custodial, over the years I had made do
mostly with snapshots, shuffled
like a bad hand at cards. Here he's resting with friends
on a Vermont mountaintop, there splurging through mud
with his high school cross-country team. These photos were taken
on our summer vacation car trip through the Rockies
as we listened on tapes to the New World Symphony.
Always lithe and athletic, his teenage body conveyed
a sense of growing slowly into himself.

Now while he's off at work I am left alone
in his North Vancouver hideout. Like an anthropologist
I inspect his kitchen, discover
a different taste in curtains and cereals
and on the bedroom walls find masks
from his months working in Mali and other places
I have not been. In the bathroom a succession
of angled mirrors reflects on my father, my son, myself,
an awkward triptych. Our paths diverge.
What can I do but let go?

That evening as he prepares dinner
there is much to admire – a sturdy dedication
to the disabled kids where he spends his days,
his camping trips, skiing, pickup games of hockey,
and glimpse even now the good father he'll one day become.
And while with him I try to forget
how children, hostage to parents' memories,
grow ambered in cuteness, toddler shots, family jokes.

But letting go takes time:
I must learn to acclimatize to this new habitat
of western light and accept that when the mists
withdraw from high ground over Capilano Canyon
I am confronted with a different prospect
that blends relief and sadness, recognizing
he's his own man, part stranger, partly mine.

WINTER SUNLIGHT

Christmas exams. Standing guard
over fifty students, I almost hear
the white noise of their minds
reflecting fresh snow outside,
and winter sunlight, as I slide between
cramped desks to answer questions,
and hand out paper. Against my will
I find myself thinking of
the daughter I never had,
glimpsing her constantly
with bent head, sudden smile,
falling hair brushed aside
or striding insouciant
into a lecture room.

Daydreams only. At last
age or necessity
has forced me to pare away
the dead skin of my lust,
the Doubting Thomas greed
for what I had assumed
could become intimacy,
even love. I strive to be
instead a connoisseur
of gestures: that sudden flare
of skirts, folk dancers' blazing
oblivion, entranced
into emphatic movement,
can still enliven my pulse;
or a skier, flat out at the finish,
sweat-drenched, victorious,
holding her arms aloft;

a soloist glancing up
from violin or flute
at the conductor's baton.
These quicken, exhilarate.
They also trigger flashbacks,
recovered memories –

Hammerfest, Crete, Positano,
places I've put behind me
and may never visit again –
loom up suddenly like ghosts
to touch me and disappear.
Enough after many years
learning to trust myself
that I am content to be
no more than my role, or at best
some obsolete father figure.

In a flurry of goodbyes,
Christmas wishes, I gather up
exam books and overcoat.
Reassuming my age
and keeping a civil distance,
I am released into winter.

TRANSPARENCIES

In the beginning, light,
a drained sky, rinsed of meaning,
darkness wrung dry,
trace elements only, crevices
uneasily harbouring shadow.

Though the city's daytime kaleidoscope
shakes us through a fine skein
of sensitivities,
allowing cranes to balance
new cages around us,
and the Metro to undermine
our frantic infrastructures,
as we suffer banks to raise
gold-plated columns, reinforced
with our adoring trust, all is skin-deep;
it is the Midas sunset
we need to wallow in
when on the bus home, windows
flash out suddenly in one
luminous gash as El Greco saw Toledo,
framing an instant truth,
to flush us with unforeseen
happiness. Once is enough,
having the light shine through us,
to come into our own
sacred oblivion. We see
by being seen, and shone through
to what is beyond vision,
being at one.

It cannot last, and yet,
although at the end
even words fade,
implicitly we still
want to try out smoke signals,
sign language, as if
they could make sense of night.
Nun-like, I take to the dark,
enter an immaculate
habit of silence.

MAPS, REVISITED

I measure out my span of life in maps:
journeys I took as a kid that lasted whole days
are over by lunchtime now; only distant horizons appeal
as I triple-bypass city walls, castles, a Saxon church
in my haste to be wherever I am bound.

No time for detours, cobbled lanes. The roads
I travelled then lead nowhere, are overcome
with grass, once thriving harbours have fallen
into disuse, and antique county towns
like Huntingdon or Conway silt with my
sepia memories.

As my whole life accelerates, maps like an ECG
may record the status quo but cannot foretell
how the next decade will change, nor whether I
will be there to watch it happen.

This is an old man's poem. Willy-nilly
I'm a stranger here in my homeland, a displaced person.
When wooden signposts rot and are not replaced
I have to ask directions in a country I once knew
by heart. My maps are in tatters
and the new ones sport a legend I cannot decipher.

VOX HUMANA

1. *The Rehearsal*
Death holds us close that day: a mutual friend suddenly
felled by a heart attack. Then, through steady rain
the whole trip back by car from Winnipeg.
Though unnerved at first by argument and grief,
we sing for three hundred miles into the dusk,
folk songs – mostly the tunes, we have few words
to withstand our emptiness. At last before Thunder Bay
the clouds disperse, with slowly the Northern Lights
half-lighting us home in fragile unison.

Next evening a rehearsal for your choir
of Verdi's *Requiem*. Would I come? It is a chance
to see a different you, outside your home.
I go along. Dull the suburban church,
sixty years old at most.
In the lobby handshakes and small talk, inside
through undistinguished stained glass behind the altar
late sunlight still illuminates each pew.
The choir's ad hoc community –
bank teller, store clerk, housewife, realtor,
the local MP's dowdily overdressed wife –
soon blends to a single voice,
piecing makeshift quilts of sound from the scraps
of everyday. The Dies Irae takes off, soars like a jetliner
beyond our hearing over Thunder Bay.

2. *Venasque*
In the Midi a sudden outcrop,
bulwark of anonymous
mediaeval belief.
The region's capital once,

today it is merely a hilltop
village shuttered fast against the noon,
a scramble of houses clinging to a ridge,
precarious, history's jetsam.
Summer visitors only,
in the light of evening we reach
a stone house on the main square.

Layer on layer, Rome, Byzantium,
the past has been laid down.
We stroll, latticed in shadows
of weathered stone, seasoned wood,
their sturdy intricacies
making the simple dramatic.

In these low vaults at night,
crowded with homespun potters,
artisans, painters, students
around an open hearth,
we gather by candlelight
to the sound of a hurdy-gurdy.
As a young musician from Paris
intones the buzz and plangency
of antique song, pulses quicken
to his intricate fingerings.
Not just the rhythms move us
beyond ourselves, nor the fumes
of local wine, the sense
of pewter and brass, rough walls.
This stranger's song
thrills and reverberates,
making us one within
the texture of the past.

3. *Fado*

Exploring Alfama, admiring the immaculate
white-washed poverty, winding alleys and stairways
of Lisbon's oldest quarter, we were accosted by
a ship's captain, who hailed us: "You English?"
Even Ulla, my German wife, admitted it. He took us in tow
to show us his city. He began with the neighbourhood bars,
standing us glass after glass of white wine straight from the cask
and gyros sliced from the turning spit, and later seafood,
but before that sat us down
in a local café, no artist's or tourist's haunt,
but a low-hung room, wine barrels for tables, tobacco smoke
scrolling the air. Urged forward by his mates
someone stepped out
to sing fados, hardly more than a boy
in army fatigues just back from Mozambique.

Though we couldn't follow his words – love or desire?
an elegy for fading youth? – it didn't matter:
caught up in the song, its notes transfigured us
with a sadness we could not shake. A single throat
and grainy fingers on guitar strings united us
with all who heard it. Finished, he melted back
into his friends, but not before the songs
had imprinted that place on mind and memory.

4. *An die Musik*

On the overnight express from Helsinki to Rovaniemi
the engine's smoke tangled in moonlight, billowing over
half-seen forests and meadows,
the train's steady sway and shudder accompanied by
a crescendo of women's voices from the next coach,
singing hymns to ward off the darkness. A church choir maybe,
or some evangelical group. I never saw them
but this, my first night in Finland, not knowing the language

I let their harmonies bear me along
to my unknown destination.
                        So too, near Sarajevo,
sitting alone under shade trees in a beer garden
with a suckling pig roasting over an open pit and a tankard
                                                    to hand,
I heard a folk singer, her voice rising high above
the hubbub of traffic, small talk at the neighbouring tables,
with sounds I had never imagined before,
a voice distilled
from mute centuries of hidden suffering
and hints of a darkness about to begin again.
And fifteen years back in Jaisalmer, at the edge
of the Thar desert, a wizened cross-legged man
coaxed from his one-string fiddle for me, sole auditor,
a far, unheard-of music, his cracked voice singing along.
Wherever I go, Romania, Hungary
the music follows. These moments lodge
in unexplored reaches of memory, mingle with
the citizens' choruses in Boris Godunov,
plainchant at Tewkesbury Abbey, campfire songs
after the floods in Zeeland, everywhere
I sense them, these subterranean wells.
It is the human voice claims us, world music telling us
we are one beyond language, and for a while at least
can abandon our sadness for joy.

THE LAND OF WHAT IF

Though it comes across as absent-mindedness,
the heart is at stake:
an affair that came between them
two decades back, a job offer not taken
in a distant, exciting city, a loved son
dead at twenty.

"Don't go there," consoling friends said,
"That's all in the past,
water under the bridge." But nothing
leaves without trace. He catches himself in a sigh;
she, brushing white hair, thinks what she might have been
in another country.

So they did go there, became
permanent residents, invalids lost for words
in the land of what if.

REASONABLE ACCOMMODATION

First off, presumably, a crib until
I outgrew it, and was granted
my own space where I gathered
around me a cornucopia
of parents, stuffed animals, toy trains.
At twenty I graduated
to a room of my own in college,
then, after marriage, a whole house
with enough space for children constantly
growing their own needs. Divorces (twice)
meant each time haphazardly starting
afresh in apartments until,
semi-detached, in a good neighbourhood,
for nine years a matrimonial home.
Then as the children left,
a townhouse, one of six, overlooking a river
and tennis courts. For seventeen years,
we built up equity, a brief taste
of ownership and all its woes.
Now at last with lock, stock, and barrel
secured in self-storage units,
our caravan reaches Samarkand, we rest
in modest comfort by the abiding ocean
until presumably such time
when, 'each according to his need',
I come into my own, a plain pine box,
no lawyers wanted here, no title deeds,
in perpetuity.

BEQUEST

I lie awake: no big city white noise here.
At most a late returning cyclist contests
the claims of silence, then unexpected snow,
ticking across the window panes as softly
as the ash of Europe's history.

Most of the folk I knew
in the volunteer work camps have died,
moved on, assumed other names. I survive
fifty years later only by
a thread of memory.

My travelling clock's unadjusted,
Ottawa time. Here it is 2 a.m.
I turn on the bedside lamp. Weigh up
my assets: memories, an eye
for classical proportion, tall eighteenth-century windows,
an affection for certain trees, birds, animals,
a love for this or that composer, painter, – nothing
I can pass on. If I died now, who could re-assemble
the shards of my past, and how might I bequeath
the simple happiness I felt
admiring old archways, courtyards, the abbey's carillon,
or strolling beside an elegant canal? At the end of the day
so little to bequeath.

LANGUAGE TRAINING

Who can translate the language of death? Its hieroglyphics
are a Finnish of the soul. Like the lions of Venice in war-time
its books are closed to us, its grammar
unbearably difficult. I only know
when I approach strangers,
no one can answer my questions
in words I can understand. There is a randomness
to its syntax and ironic inflections.

Last week in a second-hand bookstore
I picked up a Teach Yourself Death,
but it's hard to learn on your own
when there are no native speakers.

FIFTEEN NOCTURNES

1

Evening lies fallow: afternoon's harvest of noise
has been gathered in, sheaves of sunlight stowed
in a dark barn. The estuary's glutted with gold,
the total sky august, mysterious.

2

Textures of light; beyond
an elusive flotsam of cloud
richer darkness prevails
among the salt marshes, extends
deserted shorelines.

3

The skies grow lucid,
jet trails ruffle then merge
into mares' tails, cirrostratus.
High winds up there. Down here
after a close day, relief.
Our local park's staked out
with panels of shadow.
A few lamps cautiously peer
into encroaching darkness.
Come what may, I am at ease
making my peace with night.

4
I sit on the deck as though
by merely observing the gradual
diminishing of light
I might somehow halt the erosion,
staunch the transfusion of darkness
into my veins, as though
I could change something.
Acquiescence is all. Soon I must go inside,
leave lawn chairs to their own devices.
Shade overwhelms me, it is too dark to read.

5
Already on the outskirts indigo overlays,
deletes, the pretence of order.
Day's colours start to run, soon rooflines
will recede and all the carefully tended
parklands will be swallowed, ingested
into the maw of darkness.
Even while light remains
nostalgia like algae entangles us,
drifts over the placid lake where, listen!
the marsh is obsessed with birds.

6

Do I grow too fond of the dusk
with its veiled elusive half-lights
and hide-and-seek lakeshore voices
disturbing the foliage, children
who will not let go, who want their day
to last forever? Alone,
I indulge this velvet calm,
colour's slow fade-out from the kitchen garden,
and am resolved, content
how the skyline's edges blur
and birdsong diminishes.
I am herded into, welcome,
the coldharbour of sleep.

7

Dusk cross-hatches the trees,
just beyond earshot meadows and waterways
glisten with animals
that slink through reeds and root
for scents of home.
Ensconced in my drawing-room,
watching the world remotely on TV,
I am freed from all this till nothing
can overwhelm my prized
security.

8

As truck headlamps lance the twilight,
shadow transients converge
briefly, then melt back
into the undergrowth.
Beyond my French windows, on the patio,
birds still secure in Summer
ignore the Fall crimson.
In silence I receive
the absolution of darkness.

9

Darkness confers on the forest a letting-go,
a slow dispersal of form, reducing its shapes
into an easeful wilderness. We walk
attentive to silences, carry our own calm
before us like lanterns.

10

Feral flutter of wing, flash of claw
rips the silence apart.
Interrupted dreams
persist in their half-life, never
truly erased from consciousness,
sometimes re-appear
to shadow our everyday.

11
Thoughts like deer startled
leap out of dappled cover
into the full glare
of headlights, freeze-
framed in darkness.
Later while we sleep uneasily
night creatures pursue
their devious purposes, explore
rotted tree stumps, cool burrows,
another universe.

12
Across the river distant lights tantalize:
a mirage of dawn, a lamplit diaspora,
settles suburban hillsides
with discredited dreams
of community.
The sounds of night make up no unison
but break down into traffic, tavern brawls,
fire-trucks, police car sirens.
Only in this garden, sanctuary –
for hopes absolved, for death, for dissolution.
Among these roots we can breathe easier,
become ourselves again.

13
Never enamoured of the night,
I crave the dawn's first unfolding
of hidden colour, the flags run up, the sluice
of daylight flooding the water meadows
and the sky at least for now a confident blue
I know will not last. Curtains drawn back,
I welcome autumn's warm hand on my sleeve,
and seek imagined peace.

14
How can we read the night?
Illiterate
to any final meaning,
I wake and scan by moonlight
the scrawl of a jet stream's
all but illegible message,
holding it up against
the trees' calligraphy.
How do I encrypt
these petrograph graffiti
that do not outlast the minute
and cannot illuminate
such absolute blackness?
Night leaves me no choice.
I must believe in morning.

15
Daylight elucidates
tarpaper shack and jetty, seaweed and foam.
The siege is lifted. Once again
I take the landscape at face value,
I am for now home free.

Acknowledgements

Some of these poems have been published in the following periodicals: *Algonquin Roundtable Review, The Antigonish Review, Ariel, Border Crossings, Canadian Forum, Canadian Journal of Netherlandic Studies, Canadian Literature, Cyphers* (Ireland), *The Dalhousie Review, The Fiddlehead, Harpweaver, The New Quarterly, Orbis* (UK), *CJ Outlook, Our Times, PN Review* (UK), *Prairie Fire, Queen's Quarterly,* and *Takahe* (NZ); in the chapbook *Habitat* (Alfred Gustav Press, North Vancouver, 2009); and in three anthologies, *Rocksalt, Symbiosis,* and *Celebrating Poets over Seventy.*

OTHER QUATTRO POETRY BOOKS